ENDORSEMENTS

The Economic Liberty Book is perfect for anyone that wants to learn basic Bible teaching about economics. It covers a wide variety of concepts that are well explained.

— Joe Theismann
World Champion Quarterback and Entrepreneur

There are many books now about our endangered economy, and I've read several because I'm troubled myself. *The Economic Liberty Book* is, I believe, the best book on this topic available. I hope it sells a million copies!

— Pat Boone
Composer, Actor, Author, and Entrepreneur

The
Economic Liberty
Book

GOD'S BLUEPRINT FOR PROSPERITY

By John Bona and Don Schanzenbach

■STORY OF LIBERTY Press

The Economic Liberty Book
GOD'S BLUEPRINT FOR PROSPERITY
by John Bona and Don Schanzenbach

ISBN: 978-0-9978868-8-7 (paperback)
ISBN: 978-0-9978868-9-4 (PDF e-book)

Copyeditor: Ronald W. Kirk
Editor: Michelle Shelfer, benediction.biz

Cover design based on *The Liberty Book* cover, by Chris Garborg
at www.garborgdesign.com
Adapted for this title by Erika Schanzenbach

Published by
Story of Liberty Press, LLC
www.thestoryoflibertypress.com
‖STORY ᴏғ **LIBERTY** Press

CONTENTS

INTRODUCTION

This book doesn't deal with obtuse theory. Instead, we offer a practical handbook demonstrating important ways Biblical wisdom can transform people and their nations toward greater wealth. With words, economists seldom economize. While the wealth of nations may variously accumulate and evaporate, explanations for it typically come with an uneconomical wealth of words. Our purpose here, however, is not to follow every trailing tendril of the money tree. Rather, we have set forth a two-fold purpose:

First, we seek to persuade and demonstrate that economic science is not humanistic or materialistic at root. Rather, we must understand the field of economics in Biblical terms. God and godly wisdom must define the content of the economics curriculum.

Second, we offer an ordered discussion of the foundational economic principles relevant to the cultural and personal realities — the needs of our and every time. As wealth production requires liberty of action, this is a book about liberty. And wealth is important to the work of the Great Commission of Christ. The production of wealth and its legal protection are fundamental in Scripture. Believing then that economic liberty is vital to a godly and free people generally, we offer this compendium of specific ideas and stories for your edification.

Chapter 1

Blessing and Cursing through Generations

Our fathers sinned, and are no more;
It is we who have borne their iniquities.

— Lamentations 5:7

BLESSING AND CURSING:
KEY TO EVERY NATION'S SUCCESS

We rarely hear great ideas with the strength to better the world. We would go so far as to say that most economics majors, let alone most Americans, have never heard such ideas. Our heads naturally spin when we try to entertain complex economic theories. Even the uninitiated somehow knows that economic texts will be crammed with arcane theories and graphs discussing the nature and flow of money and goods. We expect to read about supply and demand, the gold standard, technical details on how banks work, and maybe how banks *do not* work. They likely discuss banking history. Those books will investigate interest rates and the math surrounding them. Economics professors peddle treatises on capitalism and communism and consumerism to establish a name for themselves with some economic insight previously unrealized. Yet as materialists without an underlying moral framework, they usually never consider or offer the underlying principles necessary to a sound understanding of economics. Their work is often as fragmented and meaningless as their godless world.

All thinkers and writers on every topic necessarily hold a bias, or a set of biases, that carries them along. Many people call that bias a *worldview*. Humanists use a materialistic assumption to form their worldview. Christians use Biblical theology, a word currently out of vogue in popular Christian culture, to form theirs. Both Christian and non-Christian writers use practiced principles by which they decide what is right or wrong, true or false, important or unimportant. Those principles, when applied to studies in any field, push the student toward conclusions consistent with the underlying perspective. We, as Christians, sum up *our* perspective or bias in agreement with the Apostle Peter in his statement about Jesus Christ:

> His divine power has granted to us everything pertaining to life and godliness, through the true knowledge of Him who called us by His own glory and excellence (2 Peter 1:3).

By accepting Peter's teaching that *"His divine power has granted to us everything pertaining to life and godliness,"* we have a principle, a theological principle rooted in truth by which we can begin our study of economics. From this vantage point, we may accurately discern the most important economic principles to study. If we can determine the most important Scriptural economic ideas, then we may focus our attention to the greatest advantage.

The economic principle most broadly taught throughout Scripture is that of God's blessings or cursings. This doctrine lies all over the surface of the Book — easy to discover, though widely ignored. In poking through an economics book by a popular reformed minister, we find not a breath about how the blessings or cursings of God might affect the economy of an individual or of a nation. God, however, declares the principle of blessings and cursings critically important in understanding His economic works. We Christians seem generally to disagree, allowing humanist thinkers to tell us what is important. We may spar over which humanist ideas should prevail, but without question we assume in such discussions that God's promises concerning economic blessings and cursings do not apply. Our economic house of cards typically builds on wobbly foundations. We struggle to understand the *works* of God because we have not respected the *Word* of God.

God explains His blessings and cursings with detailed clarity in Deuteronomy 27:11–29:1. He first warns His people Israel that if they disobey Him He will curse them, and if they obey Him He will bless them. E. C. Wines explains the blessings and cursings of Deuteronomy in this way:

> The [Hebrew] Constitution contained a provision that when the Israelites came into the promised land, it should be submitted to the people, and formally accepted by them all. They were to be assembled in an amphitheater formed by two mountains, — Ebal, a bleak, frowning rock, towering on one side, and Gerizim, springing up covered with verdure and beauty on the other. The one height was a prophetic monument of the prosperity and loveliness, which would follow the observance of these institutions; the other, of the barrenness and desolation, which a disregard of the constitution would inevitably bring upon the nation. There the tribes, when the proper time came, were ranged in order, and listened to its provisions; and there they signified their acceptance of it, by an act of free choice, which was binding on them and their children for ever.[1]

---

[1] E. C. Wines, *Commentaries on the Laws of the Ancient Hebrews* (Philadelphia: Presbyterian Board of Publication, 1853), 632.

Our focus here is on the blessings and cursings directly involving economic consequences due to the behavior of the people. First, consider some of the reasoning behind the paradigm of blessings or cursings God dispenses:

> Then Moses and the Levitical priests spoke to all Israel, saying, "Be silent and listen, O Israel! This day you have become a people for the Lord your God. You shall therefore obey the Lord your God, and do His commandments and His statutes which I command you today" (Deut. 27:9–10).

> All these blessings will come upon you and overtake you if you obey the Lord your God (Deut. 28:2).

These introductory sentences emphasize that God speaks to the nation *as a nation*. These promises for blessings or cursings apply to the entire nation as a people. *"Listen, O Israel."* God blesses or curses entire nations upon the conduct of that particular group of people. We learn that the effects of our actions, our obedience or disobedience to God, are not solely of private concern. My disobedience may cause a loss of blessing for my neighbors! While much of what we do is of private concern, some of what we do is of public concern. Sin and its effects do not stay put. If the nation tolerates your gross violation of God's law in open public defiance, then the nation will receive judgment — cursings — from the God of heaven.

For just one example of God's justifiable anger against His wayward people, consider the words of Ezekiel. Following the death of the righteous King Josiah, who does everything possible to help the people of Israel turn back to God, after decades — even generations, rebuke by the prophets, chastening and judgment finally come:

> Then He said to me, "Son of man, I am sending you to the sons of Israel, to a rebellious people who have rebelled against Me; they and their fathers have transgressed against Me to this very day. I am sending you to them who are stubborn and obstinate children, and you shall say to them, 'Thus says the Lord God.' As for them, whether they listen or not — for they are a rebellious house — they will know that a prophet has been among them (Ezek. 2:3–5).

> "The nations will know that the house of Israel went into exile for their iniquity because they acted treacherously against Me, and I hid My face from them; so I gave them into the hand of their adversaries, and all of them fell by the sword. According to their uncleanness and according to their transgressions I dealt with them, and I hid My face from them" (Ezek. 39:23–24).

God is serious about His Law for the good of His people, and indeed all people. It is also encouraging to know that He intends to restore the people by the power of His grace:

> "When I bring them back from the peoples and gather them from the lands of their enemies, then I shall be sanctified through them in the sight of the many nations. Then they will know that I am the Lord their God because I made them go into exile among the nations, and then gathered them again to their own land; and I will leave none of them there any longer. I will not hide My face from them any longer, for I will have poured out My Spirit on the house of Israel," declares the Lord God (Ezek. 39:27–29).

Every nation has laws of some sort. As Christians, we ought actively to endorse and promote laws that reflect God's standards. Oftentimes His law embarrasses us. Or we may judge His ancient justice unfitting for our modern society. When we agree with God's enemies — those who hate His law — and begin to desire the same laws they desire, we set up the nation for God's curses. He cannot bless our faithlessness. Over our recent lifetimes, we have watched our nation plummet to increasing depths of depravity in both law and practice. If two or three decades ago anyone had suggested that people confused about their gender should enter any bathroom they please, the public would have reacted with derisive laughter. Prior to the 1970s, if anyone demanded a legal abortion for any reason, they would have been immediately condemned as a deeply wicked person by almost everybody. Now when we repeat the comments abortive mothers make to local sidewalk counselors, our friends hardly believe us. These mothers talk about how the forgiving God will forgive them for killing their baby. They know the fetus is a full human being but the child will be in a better place, and so killing the child is OK. The more we compromise as a society, the greater our descent becomes. The world always urges Christians to support the latest public policy as if everyone should recognize these new lows as normal. God, however, wants us to live out better morals. He has told us:

> Do not participate in the unfruitful deeds of darkness, but instead even expose them (Eph. 5:11).

God's likely judgments against a nation are often predictable based on the laws that nation passes and enforces. The laws we pass and enforce mirror our moral sense. The laws, then, are a measure of who we are as a nation. Lest the judgments of God descend on us all, we must observe His standards of morality and righteousness. The Apostle Paul instructed:

Or do you not know that your body is a temple of the Holy Spirit who is in you, whom you have from God, and that you are not your own? For you have been bought with a price: therefore glorify God in your body (1 Cor. 6:19–20).

In recognizing that our bodies do not belong to us but that Christ bought them with a price, we can better understand the limits of personal rights within the larger cultural context. Screaming "my body, my choice!" or "keep your laws off of my body!" illustrates a destructive misunderstanding of the importance of both public and private morality. The demand to "keep your laws off of my body" is often an unspoken demand to keep *God's* laws off the person's body. This means that the disobedient person insists on defying God's law while forcing you to pay the price. And this price is more than just an economic metaphor. When the curses of God fall on a nation, they are often economic. The good news is that the blessings of God are likewise.

Blessed shall be the offspring of your body and the produce of your ground and the offspring of your beasts, the increase of your herd and the young of your flock (Deut. 28:4).

The Lord will command the blessing upon you in your barns and in all that you put your hand to, and He will bless you in the land which the Lord your God gives you (Deut. 28:8).

The Lord will make you abound in prosperity, in the offspring of your body and in the offspring of your beast and in the produce of your ground, in the land which the Lord swore to your fathers to give you (Deut. 28:11).

The Lord will open for you His good storehouse, the heavens, to give rain to your land in its season and to bless all the work of your hand; and you shall lend to many nations, but you shall not borrow (Deut. 28:12).

Many of the blessings promised relate to an agricultural society. For the farmers among us, the promises may directly apply. But God clearly intimates the larger message that He will prosper the nation generally obedient to Him. God makes some broad-based promises about how He will bless *"all that you put your hand to"* and that He will *"make you abound in prosperity."* There are plenty of blessings available for everybody if only we will obey the God of those blessings. The needed obedience is a result of faith (Heb. 11:6). Without faith, we will not believe God and obey Him. Hence, people of faith in the God of the Bible attract God's blessings for the nation.

The path of unbelief leads away from the blessings of obedience and toward the curses of disobedience, many of which are financial. This is knowledge our humanistic culture wants to bury or disavow. But God makes strongly worded and frequent warnings regarding His curses on disobedient nations. In fact, He knows our fallen natures so well that in our Deuteronomy passage He warns of five curses for every one promise of blessing. He does not desire to persecute us. Yet He knows we are a stubborn and rebellious people. Unless we restrain ourselves, we will charge headlong toward disobedience and ultimately, toward death, thus ending our affairs in a net loss. Here are a few of the curses:

> Cursed shall you be in the city, and cursed shall you be in the country. Cursed shall be your basket and your kneading bowl. Cursed shall be the offspring of your body and the produce of your ground, the increase of your herd and the young of your flock. Cursed shall you be when you come in, and cursed shall you be when you go out (Deut. 28:16–19).

> And you will grope at noon, as the blind man gropes in darkness, and you will not prosper in your ways; but you shall only be oppressed and robbed continually, with none to save you (Deut. 28:29).

You shall betroth a wife, but another man will violate her; you shall build a house, but you will not live in it; you shall plant a vineyard, but you will not use its fruit. Your ox shall be slaughtered before your eyes, but you will not eat of it; your donkey shall be torn away from you, and will not be restored to you; your sheep shall be given to your enemies, and you will have none to save you (Deut. 28:30–31).

You shall bring out much seed to the field but you will gather in little, for the locust will consume it (Deut. 28:38).

The alien who is among you shall rise above you higher and higher, but you will go down lower and lower. He shall lend to you, but you will not lend to him; he shall be the head, and you will be the tail (Deut. 28:43–44).

These promised curses, like the promised blessings, are often economic in nature. When verse 29 promises, *"you will not prosper in your ways; but you shall only be oppressed and robbed continually,"* that is clearly an economic consideration. Whatever may happen on the supply side of the economy, the outright curses of God will bleed it all away. Calculating those promised effects on a hand-held device will not be possible, yet the losses will be real. The Biblical conversation about blessing and cursing is not primarily mathematical. It is moral. This may distress us a bit, because the surrounding culture invests economics with math and mathematic formulas as a primary concept. In the real world where God blesses and curses, we find that the sovereignty of God and morals trump math. Economic success for any nation begins with obedience to God — meaning: moral choices.[2]

---

[2] We think we are "basically good" and deserve good things. But we evaluate ourselves based on our own man-made principles instead of God's revealed ones. *"They have all turned aside, together they have become corrupt; There is no one who does good, not even one"* (Ps. 14:3).

Chapter 2

Why Prosperity is Generational

The counsel of the Lord stands forever,
The plans of His heart
from generation to generation.

— Psalm 33:11

As we look for economic rules surrounding the promises of God's blessing and cursing, we see that they do not speak merely of the short-term but rather have far-reaching effects. God's economic blessings often follow family and national lines for generations. The Bible refers to this type of thinking and doctrine as *covenantal*. God concludes His recital of the blessings and curses with this statement:

> These are the words of the covenant which the Lord commanded Moses to make with the sons of Israel in the land of Moab, besides the covenant which He had made with them at Horeb (Deut. 29:1).

So then, the language of blessing and cursing is the language of the covenant. But what is this covenant? A Biblical covenant is a solemn promise by God to do something for mankind, to bless us. These covenants usually come with certain stipulations that people must keep if God will continue to bless them. If God's people refuse to obey Him and keep the terms of the covenant, then they come under a covenant of curses. He removes the blessings. This is why Moses continually warns the people:

> So keep the words of this covenant to do them, that
> you may prosper in all that you do (Deut. 29:9).

One unexpected aspect of God's covenants is that He blesses not only the people who first obey Him but several generations of those who follow. This may seem odd or even unlikely to Americans. We have grown up in a culture that teaches personal autonomy to such an extreme measure that we believe we should be able to do pretty much as we please most of the time. I am my own man and you are your own woman. We like to imagine that we answer to no one, but God does not present life and its choices in this way. Instead, He uses the language of covenants.

When the Lord makes a solemn covenant promise to His people, He intends to extend it to many generations into the future. He views the people who come after the original recipients of the promise as being equal sharers in both the covenant blessings and the covenant curses. We see this in the book of Deuteronomy when God gives the people of Israel His law. There He addresses them saying:

> The Lord our God made a covenant with us at Horeb. *The* Lord *did not make this covenant with our fathers, but with us, with all those of us alive here today. The* Lord *spoke to you face to face at the mountain* from the midst of the fire, while I was standing between the Lord and you at that time, to declare to you the word of the Lord; for you were afraid because of the fire and did not go up the mountain. He said, 'I am the* Lord *your God who brought you out of the land of Egypt, out of the house of slavery* (Deut. 5:2–6, emphases added).

And God, through Moses, addresses them again while discussing the Sabbath day:

> *You shall remember that you were a slave in the land of Egypt,* and the Lord your God brought you out of there by a mighty hand and by an outstretched arm; therefore the Lord your God commanded you to observe the sabbath day (Deut. 5:15, emphasis added).

To put these words of Moses in context, let's remember a little history. Moses wrote the book of

Deuteronomy, from which these verses come. He wrote it *after* the nation of Israel had wandered in the wilderness for forty years. When forty years earlier Israel escapes from Egypt, they rebel against the Lord, refusing to enter the land of Canaan God promised them. God judges Israel for their disobedience and lack of faith by causing them to wander in the desert wilderness for forty years. In part, His judgment pronounces that no Israelite over nineteen years old at that time may enter the Promised Land (Num. 14:29). All of the then-adults in Israel are to die in the wilderness. Only their children are to enter the land of milk and honey. So when Moses speaks these words from Deuteronomy to Israel, all the original adults who left Egypt already lie buried in the desert. The great majority of Israelites never touched a toe in Egypt nor even saw that country.

Yet when Moses addresses Israel entering the Promised Land he speaks to them just as if they all had been slaves in Egypt: *"The Lord did not make this covenant with our fathers, but with us, with all those of us alive here today. The Lord spoke to you face to face at the mountain. . . . You shall remember that you were a slave in the land of Egypt"* (Deut. 5:3–4; 5:15). From God's perspective those Israelites who had never even seen Egypt had been slaves there. This fact, in part, speaks of the power of generational character, a character not easily overcome.

We gain insight into the mind of God as He clearly reveals His covenantal intention. While we might all too easily miss or undervalue it, the omniscient God sees covenantal interconnectedness between generations. His covenantal order should inform our economic under-standing, for God's blessings do not begin and end with a single family unit. Rather, those blessings (or curses) typically continue for generations. Its reality should in-form our economic theories. It may not fit neatly into any popular economic models but it describes the way the created order works. God blesses His people for *"a thousand generations."*[3]

The writer of Proverbs tells us:

> A good man leaves an inheritance to his children's children, And the wealth of the sinner is stored up for the righteous (Prov. 13:22).

This proverb highlights two truths concerning cov-enantal blessing and cursing: The first is that God carries forward covenanted blessings of economic prosperity, by design, to the next generation. The second is that Divine Providence uses *"the sinner,"* meaning the unrighteous, to *"store up"* wealth on behalf of the blessed of the covenant who will receive it. This idea may tweak our sense of fair-ness but it is an inexorable law of economics. It describes part of how the created order works. We demonstrate our war against this principle when we demand *taxing*

---

[3] 1 Chronicles 16:15; Psalm 105:8. The term "a thousand generations" appears to be a metaphor for "a long time."

the rich in an endless orgy of covetous confiscation, as we have across America over the past several decades. We cannot expect success on the path toward national wealth if we continue to violate the basic principles of the created order. Rather, we must work and manage our financial affairs in coordination with the divine laws for prosperity. We can expect to achieve an accumulation of blessed wealth only under covenantal obedience to Biblical truth.

Chapter 3

Economic Liberty and Land

The earth is the Lord's, and all it contains,
The world, and those who dwell in it.

— Psalm 24:1

LAND OWNERSHIP —
SOIL FOR ECONOMIC FREEDOM

We're familiar with the phrase, "freedom isn't free." Oh, how true. Every day is a good day to remember those who have fought and died for America. And we should remember they fought for us, and our families' freedom too. These brave men fought for religious freedom, civil freedom, and *economic freedom.*
Economic freedom. In America, that freedom largely consists in land ownership.

With all the attacks on land ownership taking place across our nation, it seems likely that our political leaders at least, and maybe a great many others as well, do not understand the importance of land ownership and rights. As Christians, our church leaders ought to teach the Biblical significance of land ownership and land rights. Land rights are an important and continuing theme in Scripture from the earliest chapters of the Bible. God intimately ties land ownership to the self-identity and freedom of His people and nation Israel.

The Old Testament records God's work among His people. God intends a large part of that work to provide His people with land, what we call the Holy Land. God Himself calls it *"a land flowing with milk and honey,"* the Reubenites call it *"the possession of our inheritance,"* and all Israel calls it *"the promised land."* God first promises that land to Abraham (Abram).

> Now the Lord said to Abram, "Go forth from your country, and from your relatives and from your father's house, to the land which I will show you" (Gen. 12:1).

It is interesting to note that when his wife Sarah dies, Abraham takes care to bury her in the land the Lord promised to Abraham and his children:

> Sarah died in Kiriath-arba (that is, Hebron) in the land of Canaan; and Abraham went in to mourn for Sarah and to weep for her. Then Abraham rose from before his dead, and spoke to the sons of Heth, saying, "I am a stranger and a sojourner

among you; give me a burial site among you that I may bury my dead out of my sight." The sons of Heth answered Abraham, saying to him, "Hear us, my lord, you are a mighty prince among us; bury your dead in the choicest of our graves; none of us will refuse you his grave for burying your dead." So Abraham rose and bowed to the people of the land, the sons of Heth. And he spoke with them, saying, "If it is your wish for me to bury my dead out of my sight, hear me, and approach Ephron the son of Zohar for me, that he may give me the cave of Machpelah which he owns, which is at the end of his field; for the full price let him give it to me in your presence for a burial site." Now Ephron was sitting among the sons of Heth; and Ephron the Hittite answered Abraham in the hearing of the sons of Heth; even of all who went in at the gate of his city, saying, "No, my lord, hear me; I give you the field, and I give you the cave that is in it. In the presence of the sons of my people I give it to you; bury your dead." And Abraham bowed before the people of the land. He spoke to Ephron in the hearing of the people of the land, saying, "If you will only please listen to me; I will give the price of the field; accept it from me that I may bury my dead there." Then Ephron answered Abraham, saying to him, "My lord, listen to me; a piece of land worth four hundred shekels of silver, what is that between me and you? So bury your dead." Abraham listened to Ephron; and Abraham weighed out for Ephron the silver which he had named in the hearing of the sons of Heth, four hundred shekels of silver, commercial standard. So Ephron's field, which was in Machpelah, which faced Mamre, the field and cave which was in it, and all the trees which were in the field, that were within all the confines of its border, were deeded over to Abraham for a possession in the presence of the sons of Heth, before all who went in at the gate of his city. After this, Abraham buried Sarah his wife in the cave of the field at Machpelah facing Mamre (that is, Hebron) in the land of Canaan. So the field and the cave that is in it, were deeded over to Abraham for a burial site by the sons of Heth (Gen. 23:2–20).

Abraham's land purchase establishes a foothold for his descendants in the Promised Land. As a wealthy man, he knows the benefits of owning land. Though not yet the time for God's people to inherit the entire land, the Patriarchs yet clearly understand the importance of land ownership. For generations after Abraham purchases the cave of Machpelah, his descendants use it as a continual claim on that land and as a reminder of God's promises to their faithful family. Hundreds of years later, the greater fulfillment of God makes His promises evident as the Jewish nation moves into the richness of the land of milk and honey. If the nation is to secure long-term wealth, they will need land ownership.

After leaving the Promised Land, the generations after Abraham end up as slaves in Egypt for almost four hundred years. Four centuries are not long enough to make God forget His promise of land to the family of Abraham, and the Lord brings His people out of Egypt, the land of slavery, and into the Promised Land. He brings them as a *nation*. God did not promise merely to an individual or family. Hence, we observe that in God's economy physical land is a key to fulfilling God's best for people as individuals, families, or nations. Land ownership is central to Biblical economics.

Throughout the Law of Moses, we find God supporting ownership of land, even guaranteeing it. In Israel it was virtually impossible for any landowner to lose title to it. Levites could permanently sell their holdings within a city, but outside the cities land always returned to the original families every fifty years. In that fiftieth year, called the Year of Jubilee, land ownership returned to original family ownership. It was a national holiday.

We saw what the Old Testament says about land ownership. Now let's take a look at what the New Testament says. Where Jesus stands up in the synagogue announcing that He "sent Me to proclaim release to the captives, and . . . proclaim the favorable year of the Lord," He refers to the levitical Year of Jubilee. Jesus' announcement shows that He is the fulfillment of the law of Jubilee, which includes all land being returned to the original family lines. Land ownership is, then, central to both liberty and economic freedom in both testaments.

The best-known argument among those who believe that the New Testament teaches socialism comes from the Book of Acts, Chapter 4. We may sympathetically regard the many uninformed Christians who argue the Bible teaches socialism. Harder to accept is what we heard a well-known and presumably Biblically accomplished pastor say on a radio program. He argued in the strongest terms from this passage that the Bible teaches socialism.

Liberal, uninformed Christians — even pastors — argue their case on this text:

> And the congregation of those who believed were of one heart and soul; and not one of them claimed that anything belonging to him was his own, but all things were common property to them. . . .
>
> For there was not a needy person among them, for all who were owners of land or houses would sell them and bring the proceeds of the sales and lay them at the apostles' feet, and they would be distributed to each as any had need.
>
> Now Joseph, a Levite of Cyprian birth, who was also called Barnabas by the apostles (which translated means Son of Encouragement), and who owned

a tract of land, sold it and brought the money and laid it at the apostles' feet (Acts 4: 32, 34–37).

To answer these folks, first remember the loose-as-a-cannon-on-a-rolling-deck foundation of socialism. The loose cannon cannot properly perform its function, but is rather dangerous to those it supposedly serves. In socialism the government owns and controls the land through regulations and taxes, and so absolutely controls the basic means of economic production. Such power is dangerous in the hands of sinful men.

Socialism requires that all land belongs to everyone. That the government will somehow enforce this is manifest absurdity. Then, the all-powerful humanist government will somehow perfectly and justly manage all land for its citizens. In reality, socialism creates a downward spiral of failure 100 percent of the time.

Granting that the disciples did voluntarily place their material wealth into common holding, nowhere does Scripture command possession in common. And even here, no one compelled such common ownership. Lastly, this experiment in communal wealth may have resulted directly from persecution of the Christian faith — a survival strategy.

Further, consider rather Acts 5:1–2, where we learn that husband and wife Ananias and Sapphira owned some land and sold it, but they only offered a percentage of the funds to the apostles. Reading further, we see that Apostle Peter realizes their sin and reads them the riot act, so to speak. Peter asks them why they lied to the Holy Spirit and kept a percentage of the sale proceeds.

Even after the sale of Ananias and Sapphira's land, the Apostle Peter says, "Was it not in your own power?" Yes! The funds from the sale belonged to the property owners, not the government. Ananias and Sapphira's crime was not in failing to give all the funds to the apostles; it was in lying to cover hypocrisy — essentially lying to God (Acts 5:4).

As the Old Testament does, so the New Testament Scripture also teaches private property ownership. "While it remained, was it not your own?" Private property diametrically opposes socialism.

Robert Winthrop clearly demonstrated the evil of socialism when he delivered a speech at the annual meeting of the Massachusetts Bible Society in Boston. He said:

> All societies of men must be governed in some way or other. The less they may have of stringent State Government, the more they must have of individual self-government. The less they rely on public law or physical force, the more they must rely on private moral restraint. Men, in a word, must necessarily be controlled, either by a power within them, or by a power without them; either by the word of

God, or by the strong arm of man; either by the
Bible, or by the bayonet.[4]

Socialism is a real disaster everywhere it has been
tried, and it's awful for the people where it exists today.
Do you know what *nazi* means? It is an abbreviation
for National Socialism. The USSR sang the same song,
with slightly different lyrics. It was the Union of Soviet
Socialist Republics. And it was absurd to call them
republics.

When liberals pound the pavement for social justice they really are making a strong demand that the
government take your hard-earned money (by force if
necessary) to pay for some so-called benevolent cause
— socialism. Liberals always need a cause. The great
contradiction is that corporate government entrusted
with the coercive force necessary to provide corrective
justice cannot provide a positive benevolence or charity
as does an individual with a heart of compassion. If it
were even possible, history proves that it simply never
happens.

Rus Walton said it clearly: "Government is not a
producer, it's a taxer, and a spender. Every dollar spent
by the public sector is a dollar the government must take
from the private sector, from the workers, and earners

---

[4] Gary DeMar, *America's Christian History: The Untold Story*
(Powder Springs, GA: American Vision, Inc., 2010), 192.

and investors. The dollar taken by government cannot be spent or invested by that productive private sector."[5]

If someone wishes to donate their land or money to some good charity or ministry, God bless them. The decision at their discretion is pure charity. But when the government demands your money for some supposed good cause, it is not charity. It is compulsory and a tax, not a gift. Like it or not, your only options are to pay the tax or pay the penalty.

[5] Rus Walton, *One Nation Under God* (Nashville: Thomas Nelson, Inc., 1987), 96.

Chapter 4

Land Zoning
Mechanism to Destroy Economic Liberty

You shall not covet your neighbor's house;
you shall not covet your neighbor's wife
or his male servant or his female servant
or his ox or his donkey or anything
that belongs to your neighbor.

— Exodus 20:17

One practice by civil government most destructive of economic liberty is that of *land zoning.*[6] With zoning, local governments decide permitted use of land by owners — determining various purposes in various places — according to some master plan. City councils or county boards decide that certain tracts of land should

---

[6] Another destructive government practice is that of property tax. We will not deal with the subject here, except to point out that property tax essentially reduces a land owner to that of vassal or serf. If the government can confiscate land due to non-payment, the government, in reality, *owns* that land, just as a mortgage holder does.

be limited to uses the government decides are best. Some land may be zoned only for housing, for industrial usage, or only as farmland. Zoning is often quite specific, breaking down allowed usages into a myriad of tight categories, such as occupancy numbers or building density. This system, though supposed to improve the quality of life for citizens, is both unbiblical and oppressive. It cannot achieve its goals and often causes more problems than it solves. From actual events, here is a first-hand story that demonstrates how destructive zoning laws and committees often are.[7]

> We recently attempted to open a business. We identified a suitable fifteen-acre parcel. The property was improved, but run down, and had been without a user for over a decade. This blighted property lay within the city limits.
>
> After several visits to the property, we determined significant investment was necessary to clean up and make necessary improvements to open the business. We met with city officials on two separate occasions and proposed our use. The city officials consulted a thick book of the applicable codes and ordinances at the meeting and candidly said, "We don't like your use but can't stop it. The zoning code allows your use." Our proposal included

---

[7] We have withheld names and places to protect the innocent from possible retribution.

cleaning up and making necessary improvements to a blighted property that had been vacant for ten years, and adding fifty new jobs in a community that desperately needs jobs. Unfortunately, it seems reasonable to conclude the city's high crime rate relates to its high unemployment.

Based upon the clearly perceived approval the city staff gave during the two meetings, our company paid a significant price to professional consultants to prepare an extensive economic feasibility study, an updated survey, and detailed engineering and construction plans, not to mention legal advice with significant fees. After submitting the required plans to the city staff, they wrongfully issued a flat denial. The zoning district did not permit our proposed use. This diametrically opposed the response we received during the initial meetings. They could have initially told us the truth that they would not approve our project, and we would have saved significant dollars and months of time. Of course, the land-use laws insulate government employees from legal liability.

Our only option once they issued this denial was an appeal to a kangaroo-type planning and zoning board that took their cues from the same city staff. Frankly, many members were rude to our company executives and outside professional staff who proposed the project during the appeal. Some of the members even made it seem they would only approve a business use *they liked* for the parcel, notwithstanding what the ordinances allow. The city ultimately denied their own code, while preventing a vacant and blighted property from being cleaned up. In the process, they squashed the creation of new jobs. One amazing statement illustrates the mindset of many supposed civil servants. During one of the meetings the community director actually said, "Fifty jobs is nothing."

This is just one example among many where a local government oppresses its citizens and incrementally erodes economic liberty. This system, virtually universal in the United States, opposes both Testaments of the Bible and our nation's Constitution. This tyrannical action is wrong and must stop. Like many other cities in America, these city officials forgot we citizens hired them to serve the people, not oppress them. It's no wonder that this small city remains littered with run-down properties with a high unemployment and crime rate compared to its peer cities in the area.

This company's experience highlights several problems connected with zoning in general. Since readers often like lists:

1. The zoning system is inherently unjust, and encourages even more unjust practices. The city

zoning staff was not even willing to work within their own laws. They apparently were not willing simply to enforce the law, but denied a perfectly legal request based on personal preference.

2. The city staff arrogantly decided that a mere fifty jobs were not worth bringing into the community. They thus made themselves arbiters over jobs creation as well as property development.

3. The zoning staff arbitrarily determined that the city residents would be better off living with the useless, run-down, existing property than a legitimate business that could have cleaned up the lot without public expense and served the citizens.

4. The zoning law and its enforcement damaged this company's finances. The city caused unnecessary losses through wasted development and legal costs.

5. The zoning law and its enforcement damaged this company's potential profits by limiting access to what the owners believed to be a viable market. The business assumed the risks. Furthermore, profits from a successful business would have returned into the economy as either

further investment in other productive endeavors or as consumer spending.

6. The zoning department arbitrarily prohibited local consumers from accessing a needed service this company would have offered.

7. The zoning law and its enforcement reduced potential tax receipts for the city, thus increasing the need for higher per capita tax rates.

8. The zoning law and its enforcement effectively turned the city and this department's employees into thieves, with this company and city residents the victims.

Each of these points demonstrates injustice and the general immorality found in the enforcement of such laws. This story is not unusual. Citizens who want to exercise economic liberty by developing land or businesses run into similar struggles in most areas of our nation. Insofar as governments steal our liberties, we become slaves, and the civil authorities who make such laws become our masters. The citizens may have elected the authorities, but tyranny by the majority is tyranny just the same.

Zoning is a practice unknown in Scripture. We search God's law in vain to find a single affirmation of it.

We suggest that it violates a myriad of Biblical precepts including several of the Ten Commandments (Exod. 20:1–17). These include:

The first commandment: **You shall have no other gods before Me** (v. 3).

By enforcing its own preferences for land use on rightful landowners, civil government zoning laws attempt to make government the highest authority over the land, including over God Himself. The Lord God Himself said, *"The earth is the* Lord's *and all it contains"* (Ps. 24:1; see also Exod. 19:5). God has clearly established Himself as the true titleholder to all land. Civil governments imposing zoning laws jump the line, so to speak. First, they jump over the earthly titleholder and then right on over the heavenly one. They exercise more authority than God Himself, who leaves the use of all property up to the earthly owner as long as the usage does not harm another in violation of God's law. We sinful people are often so certain our ideas are better than God's ideas that we refuse to leave management of this world in His hands. We can think of an endless string of arguments as to why we simply *must* take control of events that God did not permit us to meddle with. Zoning is one area we would wisely leave to Divine Providence.

The eighth commandment: **You shall not steal** (v. 15).

Most of us agree it is morally wrong to take other people's possessions without making payment. Certainly, we think it wrong in others to take our stuff! For some reason however, we do not protest much over the civil government using zoning laws to steal from us. Make no mistake — zoning is certainly theft. It is theft on a grand scale. When an area zoned for residential housing stops local businesses from expanding into that land, home-owners, for lack of local amenities, lose both convenience and the resale value of their property. Zoning also robs the business that cannot expand its potential profits for lack of needed space in the right location. Laws restrict-ing land use to agriculture rob its owners of potential profits from developing that land. If a farmer's slough is zoned as a slough then the farmer cannot develop the slough into a cattle pond. In a bramble thicket zoned as a park, nobody can use the land for anything. It becomes nothing but a place to throw old tires. Thus, a nearly use-less piece of land takes on a *negative* value. It costs more to clean up the land than what it was originally worth.

The value of a particular parcel of land may increase with zoning. Even in this case however, the owner of the land has had his usage of the land restricted and thus sto-len from him. If you want to pass along a plot of land to your grandchild to build a home and the city then zones the land for an asphalt factory, a theft has taken place. Though perhaps not a financial one, in removing choice it remains theft.

The tenth commandment: ***You shall not covet*** (v. 17).

The full text reads, *"You shall not covet your neighbor's house; you shall not covet your neighbor's wife or his male servant or his female servant or his ox or his donkey or anything that belongs to your neighbor."*

With so many *or's, your's,* oxen and donkeys, we may miss the all-important *"or anything that belongs to your neighbor."* This would include coveting your neighbor's land or *control* of his land. This is what we wickedly want. We want to control land usage to produce results *we* think best. Instead of trusting God to work out the results of human culture, we covet that control. We believe God's seeming hands-off approach will lead to all sorts of problems. We think *we* must defend against apparent abuse ahead of time with regulation. Zoning is a tool to enforce our covetous, faithless philosophy. We cannot demand to their faces that everyone comply with our desires for land-use. Zoning provides a way to pursue our coveted control while appearing respectable.

In addition, zoning encourages another kind of coveting. Higher property values and potential profit inherent in certain land-use zones — such as high-density development — clearly encourage corruption in government as some property owners may seek to pay influence — bribes — for a privileged zone and a higher return of investment.

Even if coveting led to no other sin, coveting would still be wrong. Coveting isn't wrong because it leads to something worse. It is wrong because the Lord declared it so. Yet coveting does lead to worse sins. We assert that covetous desire for control of other people's land leads to immoral zoning. Zoning is coveting leading to a form of theft. As desire leads to action, coveting leads to theft, a straightforward conclusion. Coveting and theft ought both to be avoided.

AN UN-ZONED CITY

Most people do not know that more than one major city in the United States has no zoning code, the foremost being Houston, Texas. While most city governments would not know how to function (i.e., maintain order), Houston has allowed its citizens liberty from zoning laws for over seventy years. While there are local ordinances that specify parking requirements and other laws thought needed to keep good order, Houston has no zoning laws.

This has led to city development that does appear unplanned. A tattoo shop may occupy the middle of a residential neighborhood and a high rise may impose on small townhouses next door. People build where they believe building best belongs, where their offering may be attractive to customers or occupants. The mixture of commercial and residential properties may put off some people, but others love it. Many of the problems zoning supposedly defends against never become problems, and others can be resolved without zoning. For example, citizens can resolve differences through the political power of consumer stake-holding associations, or through the judiciary. Builders need end-users, and only insane ones would ignore their market.

Meanwhile, with freedom in development comes economic liberty, benefiting the population in numerous ways. For instance, in a tightly zoned city, employees almost always must drive to work or use public transportation. This creates heavy traffic, air pollution, and wastes hours in traveling time for thousands of individuals. These travel expenses and loss of time impose an economic burden otherwise lifted when people simply live within walking or biking distance of their work. In Houston, the dream becomes reality since residential properties are often close to businesses.

J. Brian Phillips describes Houston's no-zoning this way:

> Houston, Texas, my hometown, is one of only two American cities with a population greater than one hundred thousand that has not imposed zoning laws on its citizens. (The other city is Pasadena, Texas, a suburb of Houston.) Many Houstonians, including me, see our relative freedom of land use as a badge of honor. Whereas other cities have fallen prey to the collectivist notion that the government or the "community" has a right to dictate how an owner may or may not use his property, Houston has substantially upheld the principle of property

rights, one of the key principles on which America was founded. . . .

The fact of the matter is, Houston's relative freedom in land use is not a problem that requires a remedy. Houston's relative freedom in land use is a political virtue that should be embraced and expanded.[8]

While most of us cannot imagine that society can successfully operate this way, one of the most prosperous cities in the nation has proven the virtues of freedom from zoning. What many thought a catalyst for cataclysms has proven to be a boon for economic liberty.

---

[8] J. Brian Phillips, "Houston We Have a (Zoning) Problem," *The Objective Standard*, Vol. 4, no. 1 (2009), accessed April 6, 2017, https://www.theobjectivestandard.com/issues/2009-spring/houston-zoning-problem/.

Chapter 5

When Government Takes the Land

You shall prepare the roads for yourself.

— Deuteronomy 19:3

EMINENT DOMAIN — ZONING ON STEROIDS

Eminent domain is a process where civil government takes title to land or other real property by force. In the United States, the Constitution requires compensation to the private owner. The purpose for eminent domain *taking* is typically for use by government or by those to whom government assigns the use. The Constitution of the United States allows the Federal Government to take land for a variety of purposes including the building of postal roads. In recent decades, eminent domain actions have made the great leap to transfer ownership of land to *developers* for *private* projects deemed desirable by government.

Zoning, we asserted, has no Biblical support. Its cousin eminent domain has limited support in Scripture. The term itself never appears in the Bible, as the Dutch lawyer Hugo Grotius invented the term in 1625. He used *dominium eminens* (Latin for *highest lordship*) in a legal treatise. Though the term itself does not occur in Scripture, we may discover its idea there, within certain limited constraints.

The book of Deuteronomy records God's demand for certain public roads saying:

> You shall set aside three cities for yourself in the midst of your land, which the Lord your God gives you to possess. *"You shall prepare the roads* for yourself, and divide into three parts the territory of your land which the Lord your God will give you as a possession, so that any manslayer may flee there (Deut. 19:2–3, emphasis added).

A further explanation of the need for those roads and the assumed eminent domain follows in the next seven verses:

> Now this is the case of the manslayer who may flee there and live: when he kills his friend unintentionally, not hating him previously — as when a man goes into the forest with his friend to cut wood, and his hand swings the axe to cut down the tree,

and the iron head slips off the handle and strikes his friend so that he dies — he may flee to one of these cities and live; otherwise the avenger of blood might pursue the manslayer in the heat of his anger, and overtake him, because the way is long, and take his life, though he was not deserving of death, since he had not hated him previously. Therefore, I command you, saying, "You shall set aside three cities for yourself."

If the Lord your God enlarges your territory, just as He has sworn to your fathers, and gives you all the land which He promised to give your fathers — if you carefully observe all this commandment which I command you today, to love the Lord your God, and to walk in His ways always — then you shall add three more cities for yourself, besides these three. So innocent blood will not be shed in the midst of your land which the Lord your God gives you as an inheritance, and bloodguiltiness be on you (Deut. 19:4–10).

These verses from Deuteronomy are unfamiliar to most of us. They seem peculiar and tethered to an inaccessible age. We easily read past a section like this believing there is nothing for us in it. Let's take a short look anyway, as we can learn a few things about eminent domain straight from God's Word.

The setting for this passage is that the Hebrew people are preparing to enter the land of Canaan that God has given them. These commands to prepare roads apply to the people of Israel generally. They apply to the nation, not to individuals. The purpose of the roads is to connect the cities of refuge to out-lying towns. These roads are not essentially for commerce (though commerce is not forbidden) but to insure greater justice throughout the land. If a person in Israel accidentally kills someone, the law provides for a fair trial in the cities of refuge.

The passage mentions a person called the *avenger of blood*. We do not have much information on this person but we do know that he might possibly kill a person *"not deserving of death."* The cities of refuge have operating courts designated for providing fair trials. God's way to stop further, unnecessary bloodshed is to provide roads people can use to hurry to these places of refuge. There they will be in a safe haven and receive justice. Many of the smaller towns might be unable to provide protection and justice but the cities of refuge can.

Public roads are to serve the need for justice in society. We ought not to draw too many conclusions about the nature of these roads and all their ancillary aspects. The Hebrew word translated *road* can mean road, path, or way, so we can assume some latitude in the precise application of meaning. The passage does not tell us how they would finance the roads or maintain them. We do not have specifics as to how wide they had to be or how large a right-of-way was required. Nothing is said about road lighting or public bathrooms. The people must themselves decide almost all details. What we do know is that for the purpose of justice in society the public can, with God's approval, build roads, train tracks, etc. This is hardly proof the Bible permits eminent domain to build an unlimited number of roads, but, for the purpose of criminal justice, we may do it. It seems also likely that God would permit public taking (presumably with just compensation[9]) of land for establishing places for courts of criminal justice. We must understand that the cause of justice rises above any person's desire for unlimited title rights to their land.

In Scripture, we can find a few other causes for eminent domain. God's law specifies that outside the walled cities given to the Levites there should be a grazing commons extending one thousand cubits out from these city walls. This again is a matter of justice since God's Law provides the Tribe of Levi no permanent ownership of lands. God separates the Levites as teachers and priests, but permits them to own livestock. Public grazing land provides a just balance against the prohibition to own land outside the cities. We read:

---

[9] Given the fact that under eminent domain government forcibly takes land, assuming consistent application of Biblical law toward the *victim* of theft, the government should pay the owner double market value.

> The pasture lands of the cities which you shall give
> to the Levites shall extend from the wall of the city
> outward a thousand cubits around (Num. 35:4).

Another observation we may make from this same Scripture is that some cities had walls. It is doubtful those walls covered privately held land so we may surmise that eminent domain could secure a site for those walls. Hence, public safety or protection could be a legitimate cause for creating public ownership of some land.

We also know that Israel eventually secured land on which to build the temple in Jerusalem. We are not prepared to assert that this is the equivalent of taking land by eminent domain for the building of churches. The temple construction was a one-time project. We should not use this event to justify wide-reaching conclusions about eminent domain.

Moreover, the original inhabitants manifestly built the wall from the establishment of the city to protect private property holders within it. This suggests that this particular example of eminent domain quite differs from that of its usual sense — taking private property from occupied, productive land. Rather, the people would have designated the land for the wall as common property for the common good from the beginning.

Such setting aside of land held in common for the establishment of a community from the beginning seems common in the Bible. As an example, the public square and the common meeting house are historically universal features of communities, as in Judges 19:15. Presumably, this land had not already been in private productive use, but the people themselves set it aside for common use in the first establishment of the community. A community likewise assumes the authority to provide for a water supply (Isa. 36:2). King Hezekiah adds water-supply protection in answer to the Assyrian threat (2 Chron. 32:4–5, 30).

We would add that civil magistrates would not inherently have the power in themselves to establish such public use of property as a matter of course. Rather, covenantal association of the people themselves may do it directly through public corporations. This popular provision to the community corresponds to the public special district corporations that provide electrical, water, hospitals, etc. Such an approach decentralizes and isolates the functions from government and from each other for more ready correction of corruption or tort, if needed. The problem with the magistrate/judiciary/legislative branches having direct authority to establish public land use is that if they have some stake in the market place, they compromise their objectivity for the purpose of justice. Justice requires that those who administer the law, in their public capacity, hold no personal investment in the marketplace. This large subject deserves imaginative but Biblical thinking to provide an alternative to the common government confiscation of private property we know all too well.

What we see in Scripture concerning eminent domain by a central government is that the people may legitimately secure the needs of justice and public safety. Beyond these, we do not see any proper general use for it. Thus we take exception to our American courts over the past few decades continuing to expand eminent domain to include the promotion of private commercial enterprises, public convenience (parks for instance), schools, and almost anything government officials desire. With no public agreement to apply Scriptural standards, the people wield little protection of private property rights or the economic rights connected to property.

A STORY OF THEFT AND ABUSE
BY LOCAL GOVERNMENT

This story begins with a family desiring to open a business in a blighted area of town. At the outset they obtained a business license from city hall. Having negotiated a lease/purchase agreement with the owners, cleanup of the run-down property began. The land lay neglected and had deteriorated over years. Aside from clogged storm sewers and washed-out asphalt, a dangerous concrete structure needed to be removed. Bums were living in it.

During the first year, the business began to grow. The family hired employees and then added more. Repairs to the property continued. Family members and staff worked hard at building the business and improving the site. One day out of the clear blue, a city employee from the urban forest department showed up and demanded that the business plant over one hundred trees at locations all over the property. This was no small request because the entire property lay under numerous layers of asphalt and concrete paving. Underneath the paving ran more than one set of winding storm-sewer lines for which no one had a map. The demands of the urban-forest department required excavation through the paving, repaired storm sewers, and landscaped islands at every tree. We estimate that these improvements would have run into the hundreds of thousands of dollars. The government threatened this growing business with extinction.

After extensive and heated battles, the family business settled into an arrangement to install fewer but still numerous trees. The business survived, but at a cost of thousands of dollars per tree. This imposition would have ruined most businesses. In a legal environment where the government can make such arbitrary demands with no legal due process — with no court order or trial — and hold no respect for God's law of liberty, they can destroy family businesses on mere bureaucratic whim. Such a system and such people operate apart from right morals or any liability.

LAND CONSERVANCY

We have mentioned some ways in which land ownership is under attack, including zoning laws and eminent domain takings. Another such taking comes from the increasing number of people who badger landowners incessantly to donate their land to land-conservancy groups. The constant pestering leaves some individuals feeling they must give away their land to the conservancy groups rather than to their own children or grandchildren. Numbers of false assumptions assist and energize these groups. One of the most egregious false notions is that the highest use of land is preservation or restoration into a "natural state." Typically, they consider development for housing or commercial use is morally inferior to naturalization. Extreme environmentalists assume that the economic development of land is inherently evil, while keeping land idle is morally superior. Scripture, however, never teaches this idea and neither ought we. God has given us the work to take dominion of the earth and to *gardenize* it. Genesis 2:15 reads, *"Then the* Lord *God took the man and put him into the garden of Eden to cultivate it and keep it."* The Garden of Eden is God's example for us. Man subjected the wild earth to productivity and beautified it there. Then we also ought to remember that purely natural land is under God's curse (Gen. 3). We should recognize the importance of developing land and do likewise. Many works of men are a blessing. Under the dominion mandate redeemed man must steward, redeem, and improve all things.

GOVERNMENT LAND

A tremendous opportunity exists for American citizens to own land in America, while paying down the national debt.

The federal government owns roughly five to six hundred million acres of land, common land that long ought to have been available to enterprising Americans. Here's the idea! The government sells that land by bid to American citizens. Appropriate legislation should place the proceeds from sales in lockbox, and the funds are used to pay down the national debt. Land rushes have always worked well in America. And if the land sold for only about a dollar per square foot, we could pay off virtually the whole twenty-trillion-dollar debt (national debt balance as of 2017), and American families and individual citizens would benefit. That's truly a win-win!

Ah, yes, environmentalists will try to throw a wrench into this idea. Environmentalists have constantly used bogus "environmentally sensitive" and "endangered" arguments to highjack land away from American citizens in perpetuity.[10] However, private property owners almost always take care of land better than the government does upon pride of land ownership. They cultivate and improve it. It is valuable and so worthy of protection. The

---

[10] See the article, Darryl Fears, "The Endangered Species Act May Be Heading for the Threatened List. This Hearing Confirmed It," *Washington Post,* February 15, 2017, accessed April 11, 2017, https://www.washingtonpost.com/news/energy-environment/wp/2017/02/15/the-endangered-

government can legally prosecute — as theft against the public welfare — any polluting abuse of the land or watershed by private owners. Thus, we ensure protection of the land should any private owners become derelict or malicious in their handling of any land.

Radical liberals have successfully and increasingly stolen common and private land by designating it as "environmentally sensitive" or habitat for "endangered species." While the process for de-listing an endangered species or protected land is bureaucratically and legally complex, under a cooperative administration the government could begin to remove lands from protected lists, and open them for sale and development by the citizens of America.

THE U.S. CONSTITUTION AND LAND RIGHTS

Constitutionally speaking, the law of the land states that the federal government should not own land except for ten miles square in the Washington DC area, and land needed for armed forces, ports, and ancillary buildings, *at the consent of the states.* (Article 1, Section 8, Clause 17)

The Federal Government is to exercise exclusive legislation:

---

species-act-may-be-heading-for-the-threatened-list-this-hearing-confirmed-it/?utm_term=.df6c732b9881.

"in all cases whatsoever, over such District (not exceeding ten miles square) as may, by cession of particular states, and the acceptance of Congress, become the seat of the government of the United States, and to exercise like authority over all places purchased by the consent of the legislature of the state in which the same shall be, for the erection of forts, magazines, arsenals, dock-yards, and other needful buildings."

As for other land ("Property named above") within state boundaries —under the Necessary and Proper Clause, the federal government may acquire and retain land necessary for carrying out its *enumerated powers*. This includes parcels for military bases, post offices, buildings to house federal employees undertaking enumerated functions, and the like. It is not necessary to form federal enclaves for these purposes.[11]

Also the federal government *owns* no Territory within the limits of any State. States are members of the Union.

The Congress shall have power to dispose of and make all needful rules and regulations respecting

---

[11] Rob Natelson, "What Does the Constitution Say About Federal Land Ownership?". Independence Institute, February 6, 2016. https://i2i.org/what-does-the-constitution-say-about-federal-land-ownership/

the territory or other property belonging to the
United States; and nothing in this Constitution
shall be so construed as to prejudice any claims
of the United States, or of any particular state.
(Article 4, Section 3 , Clause 2).

If the host state agrees, the federal government can
acquire an "enclave" within the state under the Enclave
Clause (I-8-17). This grants governmental *jurisdiction* to
the federal government, but the federal government has
to acquire *title separately*. Washington, D.C. (the most
obvious enclave), for example, is under federal jurisdiction,
but much of the land is held by (titled to) other
parties, including individuals.

Here is why **territory** is not land that the federal
government owns. Federal government holds land in
trust for the states but when a state petitions to become
a state it is no longer a territory and the federal government
has no authority over its land. States are members
of the Union, so a state is not a territory.

States are independent, sovereign, and have free government.
So once a state is created and is thereby no
longer a territory, the federal government has a *duty to
dispose* of tracts not used for enumerated purposes.

Under the Property Clause (Art. IV, Sec. 3, Cl. 2),
land titled to the federal government and held outside
state boundaries is *"Territory."* Federal land held within
state boundaries is *"other Property."*

Under the Treaty Clause (II-2-2; see also Article VI), the federal government may acquire land outside state boundaries. As long as the area is governed as a *"territory"* the federal government may retain any land it deems best.[12]

The equal footings doctrine upheld by the SCOTUS, and also known as equality of the states, is the principle in United States constitutional law that all states admitted to the Union under the Constitution since 1789 enter on *equal footing* with the 13 states already in the Union at that time.

The Property Clause gives Congress unconditional power to dispose of property and authority to regulate what is already held. It does not mention a power to acquire. We may also note that *within* state boundaries the Constitution grants no authority to the Federal Government to retain acreage for unenumerated purposes, such as land for grazing, mineral development, agriculture, forests, or parks. If a purpose for land ownership is not mentioned in the Constitution then the Federal Government has no right to own land for such a purpose.[13]

The Declaration of Independence declares that states are free and independent. A state cannot be a territory and be sovereign; it cannot be a state and be a territory. A state must be free and independent to be a state.

---

[12] Ibid.
[13] Ibid.

Most states were admitted to the union pursuant to treaties, agreements of cession, and/or laws passed by Congress. These are called *organic laws*. They include, but are not limited to**, enabling acts** and **acts of admission.** These laws cannot change the Constitution either, but as mentioned above they have some interesting ramifications for federal land ownership. For instance the Bureau of Land management has no authority in the Constitution to own and dictate to states or individuals how they manage their land. It is also true that executive orders and congressional acts don't change the Constitution outside of the **Article 5**, amendment process.[14]

The Congress, whenever two thirds of both houses shall deem it necessary, shall propose amendments to this Constitution, or, on the application of the legislatures of two thirds of the several states, shall call a convention for proposing amendments, which, in either case, shall be valid to all intents and purposes, as part of this Constitution, when ratified by the legislatures of three fourths of the several states, or by conventions in three fourths thereof, as the one or the other mode of ratification may be proposed by the Congress; Provided that no amendment which may be made prior to the year one thousand eight hundred and eight shall in

[14] Ibid.

any manner affect the first and fourth clauses in the Ninth Section of the first Article; and that no state, without its consent, shall be deprived of its equal suffrage in the senate. Article 5.

Also no law made contrary to the constitution is valid. (Article 6, Section 2, Clause 2).

This Constitution, and the Laws of the United States which shall be made in Pursuance thereof; and all Treaties made, or which shall be made, under the Authority of the United States, shall be the supreme Law of the Land; and the Judges in every State shall be bound thereby, any Thing in the Constitution or Laws of any State to the Contrary notwithstanding. **(Article 6, Section 2, Clause 2**).

SALE OF LANDS TO AMERICAN CITIZENS

In the process of disposal, the federal government must follow the rules of public trust. It would be a breach of fiduciary duty for the feds to simply grant all of its surplus property to state governments. Each tract must be disposed of in accordance with the best interest of the American people. Those rights are granted *first* to the people and then to the states. So the citizens of America should have first option to obtain that property.

IN CONCLUSION

The federal government has no valid legal right to own and control land outside the Constitutional limitations. SCOTUS cannot increase its powers arbitrarily either. It is not above the constitution. Only the states have that since they drafted and ratified the Constitution

James Madison said when the government controls the property of the people that government is not a just government.

If the federal government is not limited and defined by the Constitution then throw the Constitution away because it is useless. If the federal government continues to increase its power and own and control how citizens use their land we are not a free people. The American people, Liberty Men, must have management over their own property. If we are to restore the integrity of the Constitution, limited government must be restored and be under the "We the people."

Chapter 6

How Character Affects Wealth

---

*Instruct those who are rich in this present
world not to be conceited or to fix their hope
on the uncertainty of riches,
but on God, who richly supplies us
with all things to enjoy.*

— 1 Timothy 6:17

GOD'S SOVEREIGN CHARACTER

In our humanistic age, we almost never hear that wealth
is a gift from our Creator. Yet we often hear our coun-
trymen make the accusation that riches unjustly grow
through theft of the poor. Our schools and news media
often teach that wealthy business owners force everyone
else to disadvantage. Often we hear that wealth derives
from *crony capitalism,* a system where business owners
bribe lawmakers to pass personally advantageous laws,
including laws that legally disadvantage employees, rob-
bing them of their wages.

On the other hand, we hear that wealth comes from hard work, diligent saving, moral living, and wise investment. Under this concept, wealth solely results from the work and wisdom of the individual. Yet what if a different First Cause creates wealth? What if halftruths continually repeated shape our thinking until we broadly accept them?

The following story, cut from the headlines a mere four thousand years ago, holds numerous lessons for us, some of which help us understand that the all-powerful God of the Bible gives or takes away the power to create wealth. The story begins in Paddan-Aram where Jacob has settled with his uncle Laban. Jacob has married Laban's two daughters Leah and Rachel. Jacob has held charge of Laban's herds for several years but now wants to set up an operation on behalf of his own family. Jacob begins the conversation:

> "Give me my wives and my children for whom I have served you, and let me depart; for you yourself know my service which I have rendered you." But Laban said to him, "If now it pleases you, stay with me; *I have divined that the* Lord *has blessed me on your account.*" He continued, "Name me your wages, and I will give it." But he said to him, "You yourself know how I have served you and how your cattle have fared with me. For you had little before I came and it has increased to a multitude, and *the*

Lord *has blessed you wherever I turned.* But now, when shall I provide for my own household also?" So he said, "What shall I give you?" And Jacob said, "You shall not give me anything. If you will do this one thing for me, I will again pasture and keep your flock: let me pass through your entire flock today, removing from there every speckled and spotted sheep and every black one among the lambs and the spotted and speckled among the goats; and such shall be my wages. So my honesty will answer for me later, when you come concerning my wages. Every one that is not speckled and spotted among the goats and black among the lambs, if found with me, will be considered stolen." Laban said, "Good, let it be according to your word." So he removed on that day the striped and spotted male goats and all the speckled and spotted female goats, every one with white in it, and all the black ones among the sheep, and gave them into the care of his sons. And he put a distance of three days' journey between himself and Jacob, and Jacob fed the rest of Laban's flocks.

Then Jacob took fresh rods of poplar and almond and plane trees, and peeled white stripes in them, exposing the white which was in the rods. He set the rods which he had peeled in front of the flocks in the gutters, even in the watering troughs, where the flocks came to drink; and they mated when they came to drink. So the flocks mated by the rods, and the flocks brought forth striped, speckled, and spotted. Jacob separated the lambs, and made the flocks face toward the striped and all the black in the flock of Laban; and he put his own herds apart, and did not put them with Laban's flock. Moreover, whenever the stronger of the flock were mating, Jacob would place the rods in the sight of the flock in the gutters, so that they might mate by the rods; but when the flock was feeble, he did not put them in; so the feebler were Laban's and the stronger Jacob's. *So the man became exceedingly prosperous,* and had large flocks and female and male servants and camels and donkeys (Gen. 30:26–43, emphases added).

With Jacob twice declaring that God prospered him and prospered Laban on his behalf, there is no ambiguity concerning the source of Jacob's wealth. The story goes on to tell about Jacob's work to make Laban's flocks produce offspring that would belong to Jacob. By placing striped sticks in the area where Laban's herds were mating, the herds produced offspring that were striped and speckled. Laban and Jacob had agreed that the striped and speckled animals would belong to Jacob as payment for Jacob's work caring for the animals. Certainly, shepherds in Jacob's day understood enough about animal husbandry to know that placing striped sticks in front of mating animals would not cause the animals to bear striped off-spring. In spite of this, we read that Jacob's portion of the flocks increased mightily. Some commentators have scoffed at the absurdity of this story (and at those who believe it) since modern genetics theory informs us that the rules of science cannot predict such a thing. We agree with the science, though not with the scoffing. Yes, it is scientifically impossible to expect farm animals to produce striped lambs merely by setting up striped sticks in front of them. It is not however, *providentially* impossible. The very point of the narrative is to demonstrate that the Lord prospered Jacob despite his earthly circumstances. Jacob understood this principle when he made his agreement with Laban. We may learn from this — not to set up striped sticks, but rather, that when it is God's will to prosper someone, nothing will stop His hand. God will accomplish His purposes — creating wealth or poverty — according to His perfect wisdom and power.

We do not know how Jacob came up with the plan he used to gain the advantage over dishonest old Laban. Did God give Jacob a prophetic command ahead of time? Did Jacob act out of desperation or some kind of special faith that we do not understand? These questions we cannot answer. What we do know is that in His Divine Providence God prospered Jacob, rescuing him from Laban's predatory behavior. This knowledge is enough. We may learn to trust God in our hard struggles. Are we poor? God can give us grace to live day by day for years under adverse circumstances, just as He gave grace to Jacob during his years under Laban. We may also hold faith that if we behave faithfully our God may prosper the work of our hands in spite of seemingly impossible odds against us. While laws of economics exist, we also know God bends or breaks those laws according to His perfect will. Of this, we may be assured.

INDIVIDUAL CHARACTER AFFECTS PERSONAL FINANCES

Having recognized that God sovereignly manages our circumstances toward wealth or poverty, we also assert that individual character and behavior are of utmost importance in determining our *final estate* as we travel through life. Surely, this is counter-intuitive. Yes, God ordains the course of our lives from the high throne of heaven: *"But you shall remember the* Lord *your God, for it is He who is giving you power to make wealth"* (Deut. 8:18). If that is so, then how can we assert that our character and actions are important in the equation? The answer requires us merely to accept from Scripture what may appear *to us* as contradiction, but is not. God says both are true. God requires faithful action from His people as part of His providence.

Just as we believe that God sovereignly provides, we also believe Him when He tells us that our wealth improves according to how we behave or believe. In Proverbs, Wisdom speaks in this manner:

Riches and honor are with me, Enduring wealth and righteousness. My fruit is better than gold, even pure gold, and my yield better than choicest silver. I walk in the way of righteousness, in the midst of the paths of justice, To endow those who love me with wealth, that I may fill their treasuries (Prov. 8:18–21).

The crown of the wise is their riches, But the folly of fools is foolishness (Prov. 14:24).

A great many more proverbs attribute financial success to individual righteousness and wise behavior. We may balk here as our era scoffs at these virtues as of no use toward personal financial success. Instead of succeeding through virtue and hard work, everybody wants to play the system. People of means often want to manipulate the government and law to their advantage. Poorer folks learn to manipulate the system into sending them benefit checks, food stamps, and a host of other goodies unknown only a few decades back. With our personal and national virtue evaporating, we are leaving behind the former culture of morality that used to support our financial advancement. If we want to return to a successful economy, we must return to exercising personal and national morality. Economic policy without virtue will not save us.

Chapter 7

The Biblical Work Ethic

In all labor there is profit,
But mere talk leads only to poverty.

— Proverbs 14:23

While books on economics typically present formulas and graphs, they often fail to take into account moral aspects relating to their topic. Biblical thinking, however, impels us to include moral quotients in our calculations. One of the most important is an individual *work ethic*.

The Apostle Paul famously stated:

For even when we were with you, we used to give you this order: if anyone is not willing to work, then he is not to eat, either (2 Thess. 3:10).

For we hear that some among you are leading an undisciplined life, doing no work at all, but acting like busybodies. Now such persons we command

> and exhort in the Lord Jesus Christ to work in quiet fashion and eat their own bread (2 Thess. 3:11–12).

Paul's proposition is straightforward: If a man (person) wants to be a consumer, then he must be a producer. This economic precept is one central to a Christian understanding of economics and liberty. No society can be economically successful unless a high percentage of its members produce at least as much or more than they consume.

In a way, it seems almost inane to spend any effort discussing this idea. The truth of it seems so obvious that it would be tedious to pursue the conversation. Yet our society seems intent on restructuring itself on opposing ideas. Nearly fifty million people in the United States now receive food stamps, the ultimate repudiation of the Apostle's teaching. Our system of rewarding a lack of production (not working) with an endless food supply is one part of our national economic suicide. Our nation is trillions of dollars in debt, but still considers it good policy to borrow more money and give it away in the form of food welfare. It is astonishing where the rejection of Biblical morality and principles leads. No one would have thought this possible one hundred years ago. As our theology declines so does our economy.

> My food is to do the will of Him who sent Me and to accomplish His work (John 4:34).

Jesus here moves from food, to work, to the purpose for work. He teaches a spiritual principle. As Christians, we recognize that God has a larger purpose for work than what the non-Christian world can ever have. The proper purpose for all work is to fulfill God's will. And His will is to build His kingdom. Our existence must not be directionless. We work to eat but we also work to establish and build godly rule — to disciple the nations. The Christian work ethic has been called the Puritan work ethic. In history, the Puritans transformed their world through their famous hard work and self-conscious building of the kingdom. They believed in being productive, producing fruit for God's glory in both the short and long terms. The necessity of work obtains a powerful impetus when connected to a vision for advancing Christ's kingdom.

We see this principle at work again in Christ's life when in His High Priestly Prayer He prays:

I glorified You on the earth, having accomplished the work which You have given Me to do (John 17:4).

Jesus viewed His life as one that should glorify the Father — and His work as something that must be *"accomplished."* The Father has a plan — work that the Son should complete during His sojourn on earth. Jesus lives purposefully to finish that work prior to His ascension to the heavenlies. Jesus presents us with a model for our own lives. The Lord assigns us work to accomplish. We must work as Jesus worked, seeking to complete our God-ordained assignment in the time God allots us. Christians possess a more powerful motivation to work than anyone else on earth. This eternal motivation can accrue to an increase in economic productivity as well as other kinds of increase.

EMPOWERING GIFTED INDIVIDUALS FOR SUCCESS

A plan in the heart of a man is like deep water, But
a man of understanding draws it out (Prov. 20:5).

Ed Catmull, president of Pixar Animation and Disney Animation, saw early the importance of individual genius in creating masterful films. Many leaders in our culture teach that we must all be treated and rewarded equally for our efforts. Student athletic organizations give every participant a trophy lest any poor performers feel disgraced. The larger culture is often unwilling to work hard and invest by faith itself. So it exerts pressure on others to dim the brightness of the brilliant and dull the edges of the sharpest individuals. The world insists we make every willingly dull person, it seems, to feel he deserves special recognition amongst his peers. Ed Catmull and the Pixar leadership adhered to a more intriguing philosophy. Discussing the topic of *Protecting the New,* Ed offers keen wisdom on drawing out the best work from brilliant people. Discussing how to choose new movie directors and help them to succeed, Catmull asks:

> Who better to teach than the most capable among us? And I'm not just talking about seminars or formal settings. Our actions and behaviors, for better or worse, teach those who admire and look up to us how to govern their own lives. . . . One of the most crucial responsibilities of leadership is creating a culture that rewards those who lift not just our stock prices but our aspirations as well.[15]

Coming from the president of the world's two most successful animation companies, we ought to take notice. We should encourage gifted individuals toward higher accomplishment and success wherever possible. We may think it unfair but it is not. As he contends, it is critical to develop leaders who "lift not just our stock prices but our aspirations as well." A strongly gifted individual may do both. All of society benefits and prospers when we free gifted people to accomplish their best. Solomon said it in his own way, writing:

---

[15] Ed Catmull, *Creativity Inc.: Overcoming the Unseen Forces that Stand in the Way of True Inspiration,* (New York: Random House, 2014), 123.

> A wise man scales the city of the mighty And brings down the stronghold in which they trust (Prov. 21:22).

In ancient warfare, cities protected themselves with well-planned systems of walls resistant to invasion. They engineered their city walls to withstand every artifice of war. Investing tens of thousands of man-hours would ensure the failure of any invading army and the success of the city's defense. Gates often demonstrated marvels of human design and ingenious construction. Defenses sometimes layered walls within walls. Jerusalem in Christ's age sported a triple-wall construction surrounding the city. The walling of a large city, properly handled, was not simply a matter of stacking up a bunch of rocks. Rather it required the practiced genius of teams of well educated structural and mechanical engineering professionals. Nothing could be overlooked to keep the protected city safe.

When Solomon speaks of the *wise man* who scales the city and brings down the stronghold, he describes a man of rare genius. He speaks of the smartest of the smart and the wisest of the wise. An invading army required gifted men like this, or their army would be camped outside those city walls for months, even years, to no useful effect. We read often in history of this exact situation. With this proverb Solomon illustrates the need for every society to acculturate and encourage people to develop their gifts to the maximum degree possible. While the proverb discusses strongholds, i.e., city walls, it highlights the principle that a single, key individual — well-gifted, trained and faithful — can promote cultural or national success, including economic advancement. Nations wishing to establish long-term success must educate toward and promote the celebration of individual achievement. Interestingly, in case we missed it, Solomon elsewhere repeats the concept using the example of a wise man who *defends* the city:

> There was a small city with few men in it and a great king came to it, surrounded it and constructed large siegeworks against it. But there was found in it a poor wise man and he delivered the city by his wisdom. Yet no one remembered that poor man. So I said, "Wisdom is better than strength." But the wisdom of the poor man is despised and his words are not heeded. The words of the wise heard in quietness are better than the shouting of a ruler among fools. Wisdom is better than weapons of war, but one sinner destroys much good (Eccl. 9:14–18).

Solomon's vignette, though only seven sentences, contains wisdom enough about the importance of one gifted individual that a good preacher could easily prepare a long, powerful sermon from it. We will mention only a couple of salient points:

Solomon begins his little narrative by alerting his readers to the bad odds stacked against the city's defenders. A great king surrounds a small city with large siegeworks. That small city appears to have no chance. How could they ever succeed against such massive odds? They cannot escape their predicament. Yet Solomon proclaims that a wise man delivers the city. In Solomon's example, the safety and success of an entire city hang upon the wisdom of a single individual — a poor man. With no money to buy a way out, this one gifted man's wisdom yet rescues his city.

In the realm of economics (business, finance, banking, and much more), as in warfare, we should recognize God's method to advance His agenda often includes special, key individuals. Empowered and free individuals can save society from terrible situations through God-given special talents and wisdom. Our civil government and current culture typically hate this idea. Rather than obeying God and trusting His Divine Providence through a free people to save our society from impending troubles, we turn to our civil government idol to rescue us. We have chosen this route repeatedly over the past several decades. For instance, why can't we accept the great pool of expertise resident in the field of medicine? Rather than encourage free professionals to operate under God's law, we insert civil government as arbiter over every medical issue. Every aspect of medical care — medications, hospitals, physician training, insurance — everything — is now under the thumb of the allegedly all-powerful, all-knowing, all-wise government. The result is the most expensive medical system in the world, with insurance rates racing upward faster than a titan rocket. The medical system becomes more impersonal and more overloaded by the day. Most politicians have no idea how to fix the problems within our current system.

What if our government had simply left the field of medicine alone? What if the highly gifted people God always raises up had been allowed to accomplish their best work unfettered by bureaucratic interference and bumbling? Again, some very smart people populate the field of medicine. Why imagine that medically untrained bureaucrats will usher in the kingdom of heaven or the Age of Aquarius? Instead, God in His providential wisdom creates the gifted individuals needed to advance a free society. These people ought to be allowed to do their work instead of being regulated into silence. It would be a smart move for the economy and for human freedom in general. The field of medicine is only one example. Similar thinking could be applied to education, social welfare, banking and finance, or anywhere the government-god has unbiblically inserted itself into our affairs. The economic impact of government overreach is as incalculable as the individual initiative it crushes.

Solomon's wisdom on wisdom states, *"Wisdom is better than strength."* Do not, then, look first to the financially or physically strongest human institution for help. In our culture we have unwisely addicted ourselves to the strength of the nation's civil government, the central government in particular. The human, sinful instinct turns to government as our help for every need. This idol, however, has proven to be massively expensive and ineffective. To answer the problems in society, God's Word teaches us to rely on Him first. Gifted individuals within a free economic system serve an important part of His provision for our needs. We ought to seek wisdom and wise men, under God. That is the only alternative to the costly, bankrupting humanistic programs under which we now suffer. This nation must once more learn to manage its affairs God's way, or the bubble will surely burst and we will plunge into a long and dark financial night. Maximizing liberty for gifted individuals is a crucial means toward national economic success.

WORK AND THE CHRISTIAN CALLING

For the gifts and the *calling* of God are irrevocable (Rom. 11:29, emphasis added).

For Christians, work is more than filling a material need. Some view work as what is required to live while waiting for eternity, but nothing more. This perspective leaves workers lethargic toward their work. These poor unmotivated souls arrive on the job dragging their boot toes. Lack of vision for work translates into a lack of enthusiasm. They may put in the hours required, but are not nearly as productive as they might be. They don't care about creativity and invention. They offer no extra thought to increased productivity because they view work as merely a necessary evil.

Since the gifts and calling of God are irrevocable, we ought to behave differently. The Lord has called His people to work for Him in His kingdom. We Christians must not be idle people, nor lazy. God's calling places upon us a moral imperative to productivity in work as we fulfill our individual callings. The humanist thought of this age leads to a sense of pointlessness, of aimless existence. We must resist the spirit of the age and pursue our callings with energy and anticipation for what God will accomplish with our work over our lifetimes. We should have a long-term view informed by the fact that God has determined a longterm plan for us to do His kingdom work. We ought not to yield to self-absorption and indulgent laziness, but rather, we ought to accomplish all that God calls us to do.

Consider a personal example of a Biblical work ethic in my (John here) grandfather, John J. Janas. Neither bad weather nor sickness stopped him — he showed up to work. Period. A few times he went in to work so early that he had to unlock the Ford Motor Company plant in Ohio.

With only an eighth-grade education, John Janas climbed the ladder of success. His career began with sweeping the floors of the automobile factory after school. He rose to a top management position where he worked with American automobile executive Lee Iacocca, spearheading the development of the iconic Mustang automobile.

I am honored to wear my grandfather's ring, with admiration and good memories too. The ring honors thirty years (1930–1960) of dedication, without the loss of a single day of work. And he always got the job done.

"My grandfather's thirty-year ring from the Ford Motor Company. He did not miss a single day of work in thirty years. Talk about work ethic!" (author John Bona)

The Apostle Paul wrote:

Therefore I, the prisoner of the Lord, implore you to walk in a manner worthy of the calling with which you have been called (Eph. 4:1).

God requires that the Christian's walk and work must be in a manner worthy of our calling. The word *calling* may have more than one application but it certainly applies to our labor. If we want to experience economic liberty either personally or as a nation, Christians must work out our calling with an attitude of thankfulness, energy, and a determination to be productive in God's fields and factories, for God's glory. This attitude differentiates the Christian from the humanist of our day, and our nation from all pagan nations.

Chapter 8

Economic Liberty and Debt

The rich rules over the poor,
And the borrower becomes the lender's slave.

— Proverbs 22:7

This principle remains just as true today as it was when Solomon cited it. Heavy debt opposes economic blessing. Whether we speak of personal, corporate, or national debt the result is the same. Heavy debt payments drag many people into financial slavery. Many of us try to shore up a financially failing lifestyle with borrowed money "until things turn around." A little well-managed debt can be a help sometimes, but attempting to borrow our way out of systemic financial shortfalls will surely make us the lender's slave. Unfortunately, circumstances often do not turn around. Once we fall into a cycle of borrowing to stay afloat another day, our financial failure comes upon us *"like an armed man"* (Prov. 24:34). The best solution to this curse is to avoid getting started in the first place. Once we enter a sinking financial submarine, it can be nearly impossible to escape.

One good thing about a sinking submarine is that it eventually reaches the bottom. Recall the Russian submarine Kursk, which on August 12, 2000 sank in over three hundred feet of water due to huge onboard explosions. Rescue attempts came too slowly and too late to save surviving crew. The amazing fact is that any crew survived the initial sinking at all. Deep financial waters of incurable debt likely come upon us due to circumstances such as failing careers, collapsing health, or unwise business decisions — maybe all of these and more. When we hit bottom, we wonder if there is any hope for escape. The answer is (the guys in the Kursk notwithstanding), *yes,* there is hope for escape. However, we do need a *timely* plan of action.

Remember the prophet Jonah, when he runs from God and ends up tossed into deep ocean waters by his shipping companions. A great fish swallows Jonah. In the stomach of that fish, totally trapped, and seemingly without hope we read Jonah's prayer:

"I called out of my distress to the Lord, And He answered me. I cried for help from the depth of Sheol; You heard my voice. . . .

"So I said, 'I have been expelled from Your sight. Nevertheless I will look again toward Your holy temple.' Water encompassed me to the point of death. The great deep engulfed me, Weeds were wrapped around my head. I descended to the roots of the mountains. The earth with its bars was around me forever, But You have brought up my life from the pit, O Lord my God. While I was fainting away, I remembered the Lord, And my prayer came to You, Into Your holy temple. Those who regard vain idols Forsake their faithfulness, *But I will sacrifice to You With the voice of thanksgiving.* That which I have vowed I will pay. Salvation is from the Lord." Then the Lord commanded the fish, and it vomited Jonah onto the dry land (Jonah 2:2–3, 4–10, emphasis added).

When Jonah found himself in deep trouble (of his own making by the way), he finally began to thank God. *"But I will sacrifice to You with the voice of thanksgiving."* This began Jonah's fresh start. If you are in deep debt with seemingly nowhere to go, do as Jonah did. Go to God in prayer with a voice of thanksgiving. Maybe you have been in prayer for a long time concerning your money problems. If so, do not give up, but do thank God for your current circumstances. Thankfulness is the fruit of a transformed heart. Tracing the downward direction of fallen men, the Apostle Paul writes *they did not honor him as God or give thanks"* (Rom. 1:21). When we become thankful, we reflect God's work in our stone-cold hearts and invite Him to do as He will with us — right where we are. A thankful spirit is a vital first step up from the bottom. Jonah called it a *sacrifice*. A voice of thanksgiving is the most important gift a person with nothing can offer God. It is a place to begin.

Jonah next made a promise saying, *"That which I have vowed I will pay."* When deep in debt and wondering how we will feed ourselves day by day, it is pretty difficult to pay what we vowed. The logic runs, "Why should I say I am going to pay *anything* when I can see no possible way ever to keep that promise?" "If I have already failed in my best efforts, why make future promises I likely cannot keep?" "If God did not answer my prayers on the way down, why should I trust Him to help me on the way up?" Yet Jonah did pray to God that he would pay his vow. Such a vow seems questionable in the face of total loss. This, however, illustrates what faith is. A faithful person commits to act righteously even though circumstances shout, "impossible!"

Finally, Jonah says, *"Salvation is from the* Lord.*"* This is an all-important understanding that changes everything. When we are at the bottom with all avenues for escape cut off, we need to believe that salvation comes from the Lord. It may be the last effort of a fainting heart to believe that God will answer. No one else is answering. Not believing God until our last breath may not be very noble, but at least it is a turn in the right direction. We can move forward and God can use us from there. If we are thankful with an unshakable faith that salvation is from the Lord, He may grant a fresh beginning. Jonah thanked God, and *then* the fish vomited him up unto dry land. He was quite a mess but at last Jonah was traveling in the right direction.

While making a run at a fresh beginning after you have found yourself in deep financial waters, it may be time to turn back to core principles. Earlier we talked about God's calling and His gifts. If you are at the bottom, it is probably a good time — when better? — to think carefully about the gifts God has given you, along with His call on your life. Sometimes it can be difficult to ascertain what your gifts and calling might be. That is true enough for many of us. Yet God's word tells us that His gifts and calling are sure. If you are at the bottom, you may just have to accept what God puts in front of you. That is all right. Work with vigor at whatever He gives you to do. But while in that lowly place, strive to develop your seemingly strongest gifts — your calling. Plan for future service in supporting your family, and building God's kingdom. You are then on your way up. Be faithful for as many years as God gives you. Eventually you may find yourself able to keep your vows and pay your debts. Do not give up on God.

Chapter 9

Conquering Economic Slowdown

You have sown much, but harvest little; you eat, but there is not enough to be satisfied; you drink, but there is not enough to become drunk; you put on clothing, but no one is warm enough; and he who earns, earns wages to put into a purse with holes.

— Haggai 1:6

Most of us have experienced economic slowdown in our personal lives. This chapter, however, addresses what nations can do to turn around a slowing or failing economy. Our national economy has experienced only minimal growth over the past decade or so. Government statistics, if we can believe them, regularly peg our economic growth at around 1 percent to 2 percent per year. Many observers believe these estimates to be considerably higher than sound analysis justifies. In any case, almost everyone knows our national economy has fallen into the doldrums for a long while. Here are two principles to help reverse the trend.

REDUCE TAXES

Through heavy taxation, government punishes productive individuals for their hard work. The incentive to creativity, risk taking, and labor diligently declines or evaporates for many people. The top federal income tax rate stands at 39.6 percent. On top of that are added state income tax rates ranging from 0 percent in some states up to 13.3 percent for the highest wage earners in California. On top of these are added a wide variety of taxes such as sales tax, property tax, license fees, and various city taxes. Besides all these taxes, Americans must pay the highest national corporate income tax rate in the world of nearly 39 percent. In addition, states impose additional corporate taxes.

All of this gigantic taxation conspires to defeat the Biblical principle that *"the laborer is worthy of his wages"* (1 Tim. 5:18). Under our current taxation schemes, the *civil government* rather appears worthy of our wages. The people labor, but they pay a government which robs them. John the Baptist admonished some soldiers (government agents), *"Do not take money from anyone by force, or accuse anyone falsely, and be content with your wages"* (Luke 3:14). Yet our civil governments regularly take money by force from us. If you do not pay taxes as levied, the government will force payment, possibly even sending armed men to exact it. They have armed our fellow citizens against us thus, becoming the biggest bully on the block.

If we want to live under a strong, growing economy, our nation must return in obedience to God in the area of taxation. This means drastically lower rates and eliminating many types of taxes altogether. If we will lower tax rates and respect the right of the worker to his own wages, we could see an economic transformation that would amaze the world. God could prosper us once again.

ELIMINATE UNBIBLICAL REGULATIONS

Unbiblical rules and laws have become a major source of slowdown in the American economy. While Biblical law includes only about 630 statutes, current federal regulations run to tens of thousands of pages. No one can remember the specific content of all those federal law books; but we do know that whenever we want to do *anything* the first question we ask is if our proposed action will be legal. We can no longer assume we may act as if we are free; rather we must assume we are slaves who must satisfy a heavy-handed government before we can do anything. Government regulates everything.

The essence of regulation is that the government presumes wrongful or criminal intent on the part of any person *before he acts!* Regulation represents the exact opposite of presumed innocence until proven guilty through due judicial process.

In the land of the free, we all understand that we must have government permission or fulfill its demands to:

- Be born (immediate name and social security registration demanded or the authorities may seize your child at the hospital)
- Immunize the child or risk government seizure of the child
- Prove to government that the child's education is acceptable
- Build a house
- Drive a car
- Marry
- Buy health insurance
- Pay land taxes or lose your house
- Travel to other countries
- Import or export goods
- Own many types of animals
- Hire an employee
- Expand buildings
- Drive a truck
- Collect rainwater in some states
- Burn leaves
- Sell unapproved milk and some foods
- Take pain pills without government intervention
- Carry a handgun
- Ban abortion or homosexual marriages in our local communities
- Hire workers at market-supported wages for unskilled work

- Refuse to provide services for moral and religious reasons
- Hunt or fish
- Use the wrong color fuel for certain purposes
- Earn income without filing paperwork
- Resign our citizenship while keeping our assets
- Own chickens in many localities
- Bank without intrusive surveillance
- Inherit assets without government interference and "death taxing"
- Bury your dead without permission

We could go on and on . . . Maybe we should . . . In fact, we will!

Government controls or keeps you from:

- Roofing a home without a permit
- Risking confiscation of property for possession of certain plants
- Hiring workers who do not possess certain government-issued papers
- Issuing college degrees without government permission
- Earning money not revealed to the government
- Carrying more than a couple of days' wages in your wallet (lest you be arrested and the money be confiscated as "drug money")

- Going through an airport unmolested
- Refusing to let a terrorist religion build a worship center in your community
- Carrying a firearm on federal property
- Building structures more than a certain number of stories high
- Working at your trade without a license
- Placing money in foreign banks without full disclosure and heavy regulation from government
- Having a bank account without a Social Security number registered with it
- Resisting asset forfeiture from government agents
- Owning guns with certain size magazines
- Owning guns that *look like* "assault weapons"
- Riding an unlicensed bicycle
- Mining and processing lead
- Selling firearms without a license
- Walking near a school with a firearm or certain chemicals in your pockets
- Invoking the name of Jesus from the rostrum at any government function
- Building a church without government permission
- Executing rapists in your local community
- Renting small houses to large families

The point: It is nearly impossible to do anything in America without running into a wall of bureaucratic blockage. People that want to start new businesses or expand their existing business must struggle their way through an endless maze of rules, regulations, licenses, and general government nonsense. For many small business owners, hiring anyone outside their own family is simply not worth the effort. The legal environment is too full of great risk. So formidable are the obstacles, many individuals who desire to enter the American marketplace cannot do so. We must change this. We must stop appealing to the civil government as a god who can save us from every potential problem. We must return to God's perfect law of liberty as our standard. Until we massively deregulate our nation, we may expect no real help for our languishing economy.

Unfortunately, local governments also abuse taxing power. In a city settled among the beautiful prairies of the Midwest, we find a sales and use tax department that seems set on harassing local business for more revenue. As one business owner said, "That's what they do."

In one case, the regulating department that oversees several transportation-related companies harassed businesses with newly invented interpretations of rules and regulations previously established and interpreted. This department had written the existing law itself, yet through the manipulation of that law's wording, they unjustly and aggressively audited several local businesses to squeeze millions of dollars out of them. This rogue department ignored a written agreement regarding sales and use tax policy established decades ago, fully intending hard-working families to suffer the loss and just roll over.

The department readied its war cannons. Sales tax agents went out to audit the businesses. In one case, a business manager described how sales tax agents giggled childishly as they conducted their audit.

Well, the department lost this battle with local business. Why? The business owners refused to cave in to the department's demands. Rather, the businessmen fought back, challenged the illegal taxes, and remained steadfast for economic liberty. It cost eighteen months and valuable resources to fight this case in court, but nonetheless, this time the citizens' legal guns won the battle.

This is another encouragement for "we the people" to stand stalwart against government abuse at every level.

The best answer to ungodly regulation lies in the liberty under law inherent in the multi-tiered, Biblical judicial system that serves from the neighborhood outward — with judges over tens, fifties, hundreds, and thousands (Deut. 1:15–16). Firm penalties for abusing one's neighbor will better answer for righteousness — what is right — than anything regulation pretends to offer.

Chapter 10

The Need to Blunt the Environmental Protection Agency's Powers

---

Shall the throne of iniquity, which devises
evil by law, Have fellowship with You?

— Psalm 94:20 NKJV

We have added this discussion about the EPA because the unbiblical overreach and outright abuse by the EPA has become so egregious that we believe a separate chapter is justified. The increasingly dictatorial demands of this rogue agency often bring businesses, particularly start-up businesses to ruin. The EPA illustrates how wrong theology, resulting in wrong theories, principles and laws, leads to idolatry, immoral actions, and real damage to our economic base.

Here in America, we don't have a formal, established pagan religion taking over our nation (yet), but we have all kinds of unbelief. We do have secularism, atheism, agnosticism, humanism, and evolutionism (gradual development from simple forms), all of which deny Christ, the Scriptures and the Christian religion. No matter the form it takes, whether a cult of materialism or nature worship, these folks have gained tremendous influence. They do tremendous damage when they leverage their radical environmentalism using the government.

We have already mentioned EPA overreach in passing. But what constitutes abuse? To measure the morals of this (or any) agency's behavior we first must apply sound standards. In the area of environmental regulation, Biblical ideals should inform our ideas but rarely do. As an evangelical community, we have not clarified amongst ourselves what Scripture either demands or allows concerning the environment and its stewardship. Perhaps personal laziness has justified our neglect — it seems easier to relegate our responsibility to the central government and bear the consequences. We have not invested much labor toward limiting the branches of civil government to their proper duties. This is natural since we are all sinners. It is easier to assign the duties of environmental protection to a big tax-funded agency and then just walk away. Who has time to niggle with them over the decisions they make? We all have other work to do. Our days are already full without adding another layer of responsibility — watching the EPA. If we want to escape the effects of the EPA and its unbiblical philosophies, however, we will have to engage in some positive cultural warfare, and we have to know how to draw the battle lines.

An entire book could be written on this subject of the environment, but here is a start on some key Biblical observations that ought to shape our thinking.

Of key importance, God created mankind to rule over the earth and its creatures:

> Then God said, "Let Us make man in Our image, according to Our likeness; and let them rule over the fish of the sea and over the birds of the sky and over the cattle and over all the earth, and over every creeping thing that creeps on the earth" (Gen. 1:26).

This never-rescinded command is clear. God created man — meaning mankind, the species — specifically to rule over the fish, birds, cattle, and creeping things. This is our proper work. There is nothing in this command to indicate that we should relegate authority for this work to an agency of the government. The people of our age have merely made this assumption. It is not a command from God. Later, when we read God's entire law for mankind in the books of Moses, we discover again not a breath — no commands at all — assigning the civil government over this work. This is why we ought to understand that we achieve our rule over the fish, birds, cattle (meaning domesticated animals), and creeping things through other means.

Humanist do-gooders of our time have taken it upon themselves to be the preservers of endangered species.

We have no problem with that. We are concerned about their preferred method of invoking the power of the civil government, in the form of the EPA, to take over the project. We are also concerned that whenever centralized government takes on such a cause it becomes overriding, subjugating every other concern, including liberty and economic prosperity. Under Biblical law, private citizens, citizens in voluntary association, or businesses should accept the responsibility to take stewardship of the environment and protect endangered species. Yet civil laws or regulations almost universally curtail and complicate this work for private citizens. Taxes on private land make dedicating land for the preservation of animals unaffordable. EPA and zoning laws complicate or make impossible the effective protection or use of land to aid threatened species while keeping the land's ownership economically viable. While socialist-minded agents of government control attempt to protect wildlife with heaps of laws, fines, and marauding officers, they hinder ordinary citizens from that same work through laws and taxes. Under a Christian view, we assert that all animals have potential economic value. As animals become rare, they become more valuable. This is, in part, the way the created order works. People will find ways to benefit economically by protecting valuable, rare species. There is nothing wrong with this. An economic incentive is one that will continue as long as the species is rare.

One example: The Foundation for Economic Education published an article on how the nation of Zimbabwe once effectively protected against elephant population decimation with an economic experiment allowing ranchers to herd and harvest them. The economic incentive rapidly increased the elephant population. The farmers did a much better job of protecting existing elephants than did the government.[16]

All we really need to do is to free investors and concerned citizens to work this out. It might be useful to remember that private ranchers and not the central government defended the western buffalo from extinction. The legal climate that permitted the destruction of the vast wild buffalo herds was one where no particular person owned the land. Without a Biblical view of theft, the government then assumed that if no one owns a resource, then sinful men are free to swoop in and grab that resource (wild animals in this case) with no thought for future usefulness to their neighbors. In eradicating the great herds without regard to stewardship, these men stole from the future. In this case, a laissez-faire wrong-headedness led eventually to regulatory wrong-headedness. Such theft appears subject to a judicial remedy.

Be that as it may, private ownership and control protects resources. When citizens hand over control of

---

[16] Elizabeth Larson, "Elephants and Ivory," Foundation for Economic Education, July 1, 1991, accessed April 8, 2017, https://fee.org/articles/elephants-and-ivory/.

resources to a regulatory government, the people have no accurate way to discern what the resource is worth or how to manage it. Privatizing land and resources is a Biblically allowed solution for these problems.

As it is, the EPA acts as a draconian machine ripping up the personal welfare and fortunes of innocent citizens. Friends of ours experienced the insane and unjust smashing of their efforts to start a new business in a certain city. Having purchased about one acre of commercial property the owners developed plans and borrowed money to build a small new pain clinic. Plans had been in the works for quite a while. State laws relating to their business had become so draconian that the clinic owners decided to move their business to another nearby state. Only after investing hundreds of thousands of dollars into a plot of land, getting plans drawn and bid, and borrowing one million dollars did they hear, out of the blue, that the EPA would require the building of a huge holding pond. This pond would cost an additional $300,000 and gobble up a third of their already small lot. While it may baffle any sane person as to why any property owner should have to devote a full third of their land to a holding pond, the EPA was inflexible. Water from their lot must not find its way into a creek located one half mile away. Apparently the simple logic that that's what creeks are for carried no weight with the EPA water management gods. The owners eventually found a way to fund this mad demand, but many owners, faced with similar EPA decisions, simply give up on starting new businesses.

In Florida, local environmentalists advocate a need to "save the turtles" to the point that local civil agencies have enacted ordinances that require property owners and residents to turn off the lights inside their homes or businesses. A very costly alternative is to outfit the entire property with blackout window treatments. If the "turtle savers" see any light, property owners may receive reprimanding certified letters and large fines.

Imagine living in relative darkness because an environmental agency declares that a turtle might see a light inside a home. The population of aged citizens is also worth saving. Yet they now live in danger of tripping or falling down stairs because lights inside a human's home may disorient the turtles. Environmentalists have again gone too far.

It is safe to say that some environmentalists are genuinely motivated by a desire to keep our planet clean and to preserve our natural resources. However, as with any liberal humanist, the environmentalist who functions outside the Christian worldview remains hopeless in his own sinful guilt. So he projects his guilt on others, filling his void with a "cause." This is where movements such as "save the whales," "save the turtles," or "save the trees" arise. We are not sure why these causes matter. In the end these creatures die, as all do.

We have explored only a short, quick sampling of the Biblical teaching relating to questions about environmental control and its economics. We could write much, much more relating to the Biblical dominion mandate, God's purpose for the creation, and the proper flow of authority concerning management of the environment. Hopefully, this beginning will spur our readers to explore further the Biblical perspective on environmentalism. Christian citizens must work out fair economic solutions as we labor to protect the environment God gave us. Though a change in environmental stewardship and its relationship to government may take generations, we must recognize the need to start now. Success will depend upon a dedicated constituency working long term. It is a worthy struggle. We ought not to allow the government to destroy family fortunes over swelled-headed notions that government should attempt to solve every problem immediately. We must curb the overreach of the EPA in particular.

CONCLUSION

This book on economic liberty is probably nothing like any economics book you have ever seen. We ignored all of the standard categories — the chapter headings that normally dominate economic conversation by humanists of our age. We deliberately set out to discuss this topic in the same terms the Bible uses. We searched out Biblical principles that apply to the topic and laid them out for you. This may be highly unusual but the result is a book full of ideas that relate to ordinary circumstances in the lives of our readers. We offered no graphs, nor did we present computations supporting premises. Nevertheless, the topics discussed daily affect the lives of nearly everyone, university economics gurus included. The concepts taught here are foundational to economic liberty for any people in any age. This is one of the magnificent benefits of Biblical doctrine. Sound Biblical doctrine travels through the centuries as a light on the nose of a freight train. It enlightens the entire surrounding countryside allowing us to measure with good accuracy the lines of battle for the kingdom in our day. The enemies of our faith and philosophy stand a-lit in the brightness of Wisdom's sun. We seek this light to shine in every book we write. We sincerely pray this effort will help and encourage you by what we have discovered and shared.

ABOUT THE AUTHORS

JOHN BONA

John Bona firmly believes in the American free-enterprise system. He calls on over thirty years' experience as an owner of Park 'N Go to shape his views and spread a message on the importance of religious, economic, and political liberty for Christians. In commerce, John developed property and started new businesses with his sons throughout America, creating at least five hundred new jobs. At home in Vero Beach, Florida, he founded one of America's most dynamic and largest annual prayer breakfasts, and frequently teaches the Bible. John campaigned in the 2000, 2004, and 2016 presidential elections. John is executive producer of documentary films entitled *Monumental: In Search of America's National Treasure* and *Unstoppable*. *Monumental*, released nationwide in 2012, brought attention to America's proven but forgotten strategy for liberty. He also produces and hosts a weekly radio broadcast called *The Story of Liberty,* which currently reaches more than a million people over the Internet on podcast, YouTube, and social media.

Married for forty years, John and Carol have four grown children and eight grandchildren.

DON SCHANZENBACH

Don Schanzenbach has studied, spoken, and written on Christian culture for two decades. He expertly applies Biblical truth to modern questions of culture, government, politics, and family. Don encourages Christians to influence and build a righteous national culture.

His first Christian writing sought to create interesting Christ- and Christmas-centered letters that would bless their readers. This small beginning prompted many to say, "You should be a writer." Don published two books: *Advancing the Kingdom* and *Faithful Parents, Faithful Children*, as well as many magazine articles, opinion essays, blog pieces, Facebook postings, and e-books, all stressing applied Christian culture.

Don holds an MA in applied Biblical studies and a doctorate in theology from New Geneva Seminary in Appomattox, Virginia, applied to political philosophy and government.

Don is excited to be involved in the *Liberty* series of books. His prayerful hope is that *The Economic Liberty Book* will inform your faith and encourage your heart. May this effort for King and kingdom advance the success of Christian civilization.

Contact Don at dschanzenbach@gmail.com or visit missiontorestoreamerica.com.